WHERE ARE YOU GROWING ?

Exploring the Christian Life

RALPH HEYNEN

Contemporary Discussion Series

BAKER BOOK HOUSE
Grand Rapids, Michigan

CONTENTS

INTRODUCTION

The responses received from those who used our previous guidebook, *Creative Questions on Christian Living*, published in 1967, have been most gratifying. Many found it to be a genuine stimulus to fruitful discussion.

Some groups expressed a desire for answers to the questions. Naturally, a book of discussion questions does not allow for pat answers, for your answer is as good as mine. To make this manual of more value to a larger number of groups we have included an input article in each lesson. This introductory material does not attempt to answer the questions; rather, it expresses the feelings of the author on the subject of the lesson.

We suggest that you read the input material first, possibly having each member read a paragraph. Also read the Scripture references, determining how they relate to the subject.

The discussion questions are the most important part of each lesson. There is no simple "yes" or "no" answer, so no one can answer with a shake of the head. Nor should the leader allow himself to get caught in a simple question and answer period. Select the questions which are of the greatest interest to the group and encourage original thoughts and feelings rather than trite and hackneyed ideas and concepts.

The success of a group discussion is measured by the number of people who participate. We get something only when we are willing to share our own experiences, thoughts, and feelings.

These subjects have been selected from discussion materials used in various group meetings. All of the lessons were tested in the Christian Living Classes at Pine Rest Christian Hospital. Many of the lessons have also been used in church discussion groups and in small discussion type sessions.

This guide is offered in the hope that it will stimulate people to talk more freely about their Christian faith, to share with others what their faith means to them, and to help fellow Christians to make their faith real in everyday Christian living.

1 What Is Man?

Each person must be viewed as an image-bearer of God, with all the physical, mental, emotional, and spiritual qualities that make it possible for him to find harmony with himself, with his environment, with others, and with God.

This implies that we live in four relationships. There is first of all the "I-ME" relationship, in which we relate to ourselves. We know that our physical condition will influence our mental and emotional life; that our emotional and mental condition will influence our physical life; that our spiritual condition will influence both the body and the mind; and that the body and mind will influence our spiritual outlook.

In the "I-IT" relationship we reach out to our environment. We are all influenced by the things that are about us, the home we live in, the community, the tools we work with, the climate, and the weather. We cannot escape our surroundings.

The "I-WE" relationship is the one in which we are in touch with others. A little child will learn to know his mother and father, his brothers and sisters, his pals and his friends. As he grows older he comes in touch with many others. He will usually fall in love with someone and marry. All this affects the person in either a positive or negative way.

The "I-THOU" relationship encompasses our relationship with God. There is a great difference in religious attitudes and feelings, but no man can escape the reality of God.

In these four relationships it is always the same "I"—the same person. I can say "I love," or "I work," or "I feel," or "I believe," but it is always the same inner person that reaches out. In a healthy person there is a sense of unity, and this is one of the strongest needs of man—to realize that inner unity that makes him "whole."

In every person there are emotional and mental tensions and disturbances. A person's mental health will depend on how well he handles these inner tensions. He can use them in a healthy and creative way or he can build up all kinds of defenses that will make him sick.

The truly healthy person has well-balanced relationships to himself, his environment, other people, and to God. There must be a power that unites. This is found in a harmonious relationship to God in a living, personal faith.

What the Bible Teaches

What is man? Psalm 8

"Fearfully and wonderfully made." Psalm 139:13-16

Jesus, the perfect man. Hebrews 2

Exploring Our Feelings

1. Since we have the Bible as a guide for our lives, of what use is psychology and psychiatry? Do you feel that there is a danger of using psychology at the expense of Christian faith? Is there a danger of using the Bible at the expense of psychology? How can the use of both the Bible and psychology be blended together?
2. There are a number of physical problems that result from emotional tensions, such as headaches, ulcers, or even some forms of paralysis. Some general practitioners say that more than half of the patients they see have emotional problems. Do people just imagine that they are physically sick?
3. Do you feel that most emotional problems are due to selfishness and self-centeredness? What solutions would you offer?
4. What is wrong with the person who does not like to be with others? If a person is shy and bashful, how can he overcome this problem? What can a group do to make him feel more comfortable?
5. Some people are more emotional than intellectual in their spiritual life. Others are just the opposite. Do you feel that you have a good balance between these two factors in your spiritual life? If so, how did you find it?
6. How do you overcome the problem of having too much "I-ME" in your life?
7. What kind of person has too much "I-IT" in his life?
8. How does one achieve a sense of personal unity? What specific things have you done that were especially helpful in reaching a greater sense of personal unity?
9. Would you consider a person who has a poorly organized personality to be "scatter-brained? poorly educated? poorly disciplined? emotionally sick?
10. How does David answer the question, "What is man?" Is that a good answer? Does it help you?

2 Doing Your Own Thing

This is one modern expression that can say a lot, or it can say nothing. It all depends on how you look at it. For some people "doing your own thing" means that one may do pretty much as he pleases. One may do what appeals to him at the moment, following his own feelings. This very permissive view of life has its dangers, for one is not free to do the things that harm him.

But there are situations in which people *should* be doing their own thing. It is important that we learn to think for ourselves rather than to accept blindly the things other people tell us. We can't believe everything we read today. We should not be playing "follow the leader," for this can often lead us into the wrong way. Some people consider everything they read in their favorite news magazine to be completely true, or they believe that everything a particular newscaster says is completely reliable. Such people need to learn to think for themselves.

This is also true in the Christian life. It is not

good enough to follow blindly the religious beliefs and life of our parents. Nor should we accept without careful evaluation all the criticism that is aimed at the church. Instead, we should take the time to listen to both sides of an issue and carefully decide where we will stand.

As Christians, each of us has a special place to fill, one that only we can fill. One person may be a good leader, another a good teacher, another may have the gift of music or writing. We must not try to mold everyone after the same pattern. Each must learn to do his own thing as best he can.

I like the expression that we must do our own thing. That does not give us permission to do as we please; rather, it calls us to accept the challenge to do the thing we can do best for God's sake. This is the way to mature Christian living.

The man in the parable in I Kings 20:35-43 was given the assignment of guarding a prisoner. But the guard was "busy here and there"—and the prisoner escaped. Unfortunately the guard was so busy trying to do a lot of things that he failed to do his own thing. We must face our responsibilities.

What the Bible Teaches

The parable of the guard who did not pay attention to his assignment. I Kings 20:35-43
"One thing I do." Philippians 3:13

Exploring Our Feelings

1. In the parable in our Scripture passage the man became so busy with incidental things that he forgot about the one thing that was really important. He could be labelled as "scatter brained." On the opposite pole are those people with "one-track minds." Either extreme is dangerous. What suggestions would you offer to achieve a good balance between these two extremes?

2. How do you interpret the expression "doing your own thing"? Do you like the expression?

3. How do you react to a person who says "No one is going to tell me what to do. I can do as I please." Is it ever true that a person may do as he pleases?

4. Is a person free to do his own thing even if it causes him harm physically, mentally, or spiritually?

5. There is far more permissiveness in our society today than there was in previous generations. How do you feel about this? Do you feel that people are more secure and comfortable in a permissive society than in a more regulated society?

6. Why are you a member of the church you attend? Did you select it, or are you a member there simply because your parents attended? Should one do his own thing as far as the choice of a church is concerned?

7. There are people who feel that they should be allowed to do their own thing as far as the food they eat, what they drink and how much, what clothes they wear, their sexual behavior, the movies they attend, the books they read, or the associates they choose. Do you agree that one should have complete freedom to make his own choices in all of these areas? some of these areas? none of these areas? Explain why or why not.

8. No two people are exactly alike. Each person has certain qualities and opportunities that are unique. There are things that only you can do. In this sense each person has his own thing that he should be doing. Do you agree? Why, or why not?

9. Complete this sentence: "The one thing that I can do that no one else can do is . . . ."

3 The Angry Person

Anger is one of the most overpowering and dangerous emotions. It is also very common. There are a lot of angry people not only in the world but also in the Christian community. Some people seem to be angry most of the time. The Bible tells us that "he who is slow to anger is better than the mighty." But it also says, "Be ye angry, and sin not." So there must be a place for anger in our lives.

There are differences in people. One thing will make one person angry, another thing will provoke someone else to anger. In general, anger is directed toward a person who frustrates us, when that person stands in our way.

Some people drive a car furiously when they are angry, others spank their children, some shout and use abusive language, and still others make threats. These ways of expressing anger are not acceptable in our society.

To overcome anger we must first of all admit that we are angry. Many angry people are very good at denying their anger. A next step is for a person to ask himself why he is so angry. It may be well to look in a mirror at his own angry face. When one sees how silly it is to get angry, and he learns to express that fact, he can conquer it by the higher powers of the mind and soul.

We must learn to bring our anger out into the open so that we can examine it; Then we can decide whether or not we have reasons for anger. It may be well to be angry, but it is never good to lose our temper. Jesus became angry, but He never threw a temper tantrum.

When we turn our anger inward we are in danger of getting angry at ourselves. The result is that we become depressed and lose our self-esteem. Each person must learn to find a healthy release from the tension caused by his anger. What will help one person may do nothing for another.

We usually become angry at the wrong things, at the wrong person, and at the wrong time. In the Christian life there is room for righteous anger. This is possible only when we see life in the light of the spiritual values revealed in our Lord. He did become angry, but He did not sin. Even when we are angry we should learn to control ourselves. It is ridiculous for an adult person to throw temper tantrums.

What the Bible Teaches

Be angry and sin not. Ephesians 4:25-32
Anger: sin against the sixth commandment. Matthew 5:21-24

Exploring Our Feelings

1. What are some of things that people do that make you angry? Can you explain why such things provoke you?

2. When the Bible says, "Be ye angry and sin not," does this imply that it is a good thing to become angry?

3. We are taught that we must express our anger and not repress it. What is a good way of expressing our anger toward our mate, or members of the family?

4. In the book *The Intimate Enemy* by Back and Wyden we are told that it is a good thing to have fights in marriage, but it is important to "fight clean." What is your reaction to this? What are some examples of "dirty fighting" in marriage?

5. Babies are born with the ability to become angry. They must be taught to control their anger. What suggestions would you offer to teach them to control their anger? How should parents deal with an angry child? What should parents do about a child with a temper tantrum?

6. Various ways of conquering anger have been offered, such as, counting to ten or biting your lip. Have you found a good way to overcome your anger?

7. If you meet a person who is very angry with you, what is the best way to treat him? How would you like to have others treat you when you are angry with them?

8. Do we often have "righteous anger"? Can you give some examples of it? Is the anger of parents toward a child who misbehaves "righteous anger"? How would you classify the anger in the church today? What can be done to alleviate this anger?

9. A husband and wife at their thirtieth wedding anniversary said that they had never had a serious quarrel. Would you offer them congratulations or sympathy on that accomplishment? Why?

10. The Bible tells us that the sun should not go down on our wrath. This implies that our anger should not last for several days. Is this a good rule to follow? Some people can easily forgive and forget, others cannot. How do you deal with anger in your life?

4   Can We Be Really Honest?

Keith Miller, in *Taste of New Wine*, makes the charge that many church members are lacking in genuine spiritual honesty. He does not want to say that they are liars, but he does maintain that they do not press for the truth.

We all have a need for social acceptance and want to be liked. So we often tell social lies to make others think well of us. We often teach our children to say the polite thing, even if it does not fully correspond to the truth.

But honesty is more than this, for it means that we are truthful, sincere, and straightforward in the things we say, or the attitudes we take. Honesty is the freedom from deceit. This means that we must also be honest with our feelings. Many fall short in this respect, for we often do all we can to hide our real feelings. Outwardly we can be nice and sweet even though inwardly we are hostile and angry.

We need not reveal all our inmost secrets to each other; in fact, it is often good to keep a few secrets, even from our mates. But we cannot afford to be less than completely honest with ourselves or with God; nor should we be dishonest with others.

There are several ways in which we show spiritual dishonesty. Many people make profession of faith because it is expected of them or because there is a baby on the way. We give more liberally if there is a church budget, or a door-to-door campaign, yet we talk about sacrificial giving, or giving out of love. Another form of dishonesty is the phony front we assume when the pastor comes to visit at our home.

Honesty does pay, especially spiritual honesty, for sham and phoniness make us feel empty and disgusted with ourselves. It is always dangerous to be dishonest with ourselves and with God; we are only kidding ourselves.

True honesty is expressed when we are alone with God; and sometimes when we face tragedy or danger, we see ourselves as we really are. This is also the first step in personal spiritual growth.

There is no room for phonies in the church, nor in the world in which we live. We must get rid of our "front" and be ourselves.

What the Bible Teaches

Search me, O God, and know my heart. Psalm 139:23, 24
Practicing piety to be seen of men. Matthew 6:1-6
Peter's insincerity rebuked by Paul. Galatians 2:11-14

Exploring Our Feelings

1. Why do some people feel the need to cover up their real feelings and to put up a front? Isn't it much easier to be honest with others?

2. All of us tell social lies, such as, "It was so nice to see you" or "We surely enjoyed your visit" when actually this was not true at all. How can one deal with such situations without telling a lie and without being blunt? Can social lies ever be justified?

3. Should a minister believe what the people say to him at the church door when he shakes hands with them?

4. In an article in the *Christian Herald* the question was asked, "Can a minister be really honest?" The article implied that if most ministers were really honest they would soon be looking for another job. What do you think?

5. Do you feel that people are really honest when they talk with their pastor, or a Sunday school teacher?

6. Should parents or ministers urge young people to make profession of faith? Some people say that we should stress that young people should be Christians rather than stress that they should be members of the church. How do you feel about this?

7. Can we carry the matter of honesty too far? Is it sometimes better to hide our feelings from our mates, friends, or fellow church members? Give examples.

8. Can we ever be completely honest with ourselves? with others? with God?

5 The Christian and the Playboy Philosophy

Our generation has developed a permissive attitude toward sexual behavior. This is reflected in magazines, books, movies, and TV. This may well be a reaction to the puritanical views of sex held by a previous generation. The playboy philosophy teaches that any form of sex is permissible, provided that it is an act of love.

The Bible stresses that sex is a gift of God, and must be used as such. But the emphasis is a positive one. Purity is stressed, both within and outside of the marriage bond. The sex act is an act of love but it requires commitment, the kind of commitment which is involved in the marriage relationship.

We are called on to be faithful in marriage not because of fear of the consequences or of being caught, but because we are committed to each other in marriage. Jesus sets an even higher standard of purity in Matthew 5:27, 28, for He tells us that even lustful throughts are adultery.

The Bible teaches us the value and the pleasure of the sexual act, and sexuality in general. It must be an act that is performed wholesomely, considerately, and passionately, but with special concern for the feelings of our mates. This is the kind of act that is compared to the relationship between Christ and the church.

The Bible stresses that the sexual act can be a beautiful thing. It is an important human reaction for it flows from deep basic needs which the Lord has placed in us. God created man "male and female." This means that man is not just a "naked ape," but has that quality that lifts him above the level of the animal, also in the area of sex.

Sexual intimacy is built on human respect. It is a response to the fact that both men and women are "fearfully and wonderfully made." So, we must not merely condemn some of the low standards by which many people are living today, but seek to move into a positive and creative form of experience in the sex life.

The body is a temple of the Holy Spirit. By this we must live and this is the training we must give to our children, both by word and example. Some parents find this training to be difficult but it must be done, especially in our day, for we want our children to have a healthy Christian view of sex.

What the Bible Teaches

Control of thoughts. Matthew 5:27, 28

"Temples of the Holy Spirit." I Corinthians 6:12-20

The creation ordinance of sexuality. Genesis 1:27; 2:24

Exploring Our Feelings

1. Sex is discussed very freely today in school, in common conversation, and on TV. Do you feel this is overdone? How free should we be in talking about sex?

2. If you found your boy reading a smutty magazine in his room, what would you do? How should you react if your son or daughter attended an "X-rated" movie?

3. Many Christian young people argue that there is nothing wrong with premarital sexual relations as long as the couple is genuinely in love. How would you answer that argument?

4. How do you know whether you can trust your son or daughter to have good sexual standards when they are dating? Do you feel that many young people know the "facts of life"?

5. Who has the primary responsibility to give sex education: the school? the church? the parents?

6. A rather mature unmarried couple went on a camping trip, just the two of them. They confessed that they did some heavy petting but had no intercourse. How do you react to such an arrangement?

7. Why do many Christian people feel that it is wrong to talk freely about sex? Why is it difficult to discuss this subject in a mixed group?

8. If there is premarital pregnancy, *must* the couple marry?

9. In I Corinthians 6 Paul speaks about the body as the temple of the Holy Spirit, and then lays the emphasis on the sexual implications of this. Are there other ways in which one can pollute the temple of the Holy Spirit? How does the Holy Spirit reveal Himself in the body?

6 The Use of Our Money

Today's inflation shows that money is not really wealth—it is rather a means by which we obtain the necessities and the luxuries of life. The mechanic uses his skill to fix your car. You pay him with money. He uses that money to buy food and to pay his rent. The money, then, is a means of exchange.

A wider range of possessions is available to us because of the use of money. We can spend it for an education, a fancy car, or just the necessities of life. This freedom of choice brings with it the possibility of using money in a right way or in a wrong way; for a person reveals his goals, his values, and his relationship with others in the way he uses his money.

There are three things you can do with money. You can give it, you can save it, or you can spend it. The basic question is: For what shall we spend it? The Bible suggests that we should set aside a tenth for the Lord, but this does not solve the question of how to spend the remaining 90 percent. Here we must exercise our Christian judgment.

Paul says that "love of money is the root of all evil." Money itself is not evil, it is the attitude we take toward it. We often take for granted that the people who have a lot of money are the ones who love it, but I am sure that those who do not have much money love it even more.

One of the evils that flows from the condition of possessing or not possessing money is that money divides people into various classes, ranging from the very rich to the very poor. And each class has its accompanying problems. In some areas of a city one may be required to build a home costing at least $50,000. This makes for an exclusive community. Even some churches cater to the wealthy class, others to the middle class. This can lead to strained relations in a congregation.

It inspires awe to think that we will be required to make an accounting to God about the use we made of our money. But Jesus gave us guidelines—"inasmuch as ye did it to the least of these my brethren, ye did it to me." We must give the Lord His due; we must also spend money as wise stewards who seek to do the Lord's will.

What the Bible Teaches

The love of money. I Timothy 6:6-11
The rich young ruler. Matthew 19:16-22
The rich fool. Luke 12:16-21

Exploring Our Feelings

1. Suppose a man can well afford to buy a $15,000 car or a $7,000 bed equipped with TV, stereo, and mink covering. Would it be wrong for him to do so? How much may we spend for luxuries?
2. Why does money often become a problem situation in a family and married life?
3. How do you feel about exclusive building restrictions that have been set up in certain areas? Some cities have laws which restrict the building of homes in designated areas to those costing at least $30,000. How does this restriction affect the churches in such areas?
4. Some churches lay a great deal of stress on giving tithes. Do you feel that this is good? Are there dangers connected with this?
5. The government spends huge sums of money for welfare programs among the poor. There is much criticism of such programs. What is your reaction to them? How would you feel if you had to receive help from these programs? In former days the church was more involved in helping the needy. Should this benevolent program of the church be expanded today?
6. Paul says that the "love of money is the root of all evil." Do you really believe this is true? Why?
7. Why is it more difficult for a rich man than for a poor man to "enter into the kingdom"?
8. Do you feel that the church lays too much stress on money? How often should a minister preach about giving?

7   Taking Ourselves
Too Seriously

It has often been said that we should take *life* seriously but we should not take *ourselves* so seriously. There are people who have a tendency to look at the matter of living with such intensity and earnestness that they rob themselves of the true joy of living.

All of us need a sense of humor to keep ourselves in proper balance. We must learn that sometimes the ability to laugh at a situation is the best way to cope with it. Jesus knew full well the value of a sense of humor.

Couples will sometimes argue and fight about little things. When finally both of them are out of breath, they will be able to relax and laugh about the whole thing. This can often be a good solution to a problem in the family, for some people are much too serious about their problems.

The way money is spent, or a shortage in the

budget, often causes a lot of tension in a family. When we have unexpected expenses, or have spent our last dollar although there are still several days before the paycheck arrives, we can get all bothered and concerned; or we can take a light-hearted attitude that prevents undue worry.

When you ask some people how they are, they tell you they are fine. Others, however, relate all their aches and pains, as well as the problems in the family. Some families see a doctor about every minor ailment and have well-stocked medicine cabinets. They take their health too seriously.

I feel that some families take discipline too seriously. If a little son falls into a mud puddle, he goes to bed without supper. This is the rule and it cannot be broken, for when you make an exception you make a new rule. This kind of dicipline makes an institution out of a home.

Some people take even their religious obligations too seriously. The Christian life is then regulated by a lot of do's and don'ts. The constructive life of a Christian requires that we find joy and satisfaction in living, not that we are controlled by a lot of prohibitions.

I am sure that Jesus laughed when He was at the wedding in Cana. He was relaxed when He took children into His arms. Our homes need a touch of Christian humor. We must laugh at ourselves a bit more.

What the Bible Teaches

A merry heart: good medicine. Proverbs 17:22

Amusing stories told by Jesus.   Matthew 7:3-5

Exploring Our Feelings

1. Why do some people feel the need for taking themselves so seriously? Is this a good quality of character?
2. When parents tend to be very serious about life, what does this do to the children? How can a family develop a relaxed way of living?
3. Many parents are accused of being too permissive about discipline in the home. Can parents also take the matter of discipline too seriously? What dangers are involved in this attitude?
4. How is a child affected when parents are very much concerned about health?
5. How do you feel about your parental home? Was it one that was relaxed, or tense? Was it a happy place?
6. Why are older people more serious than younger ones? How would you deal with young people who act like old people?
7. Do you agree with the statement that some people take their religious life too seriously? Is this ever possible? Is it very common?
8. Is it good to advise some people to live a bit more recklessly? Under what circumstances would you give this advice?
9. How do you feel when your minister tells a story in his sermon that makes people laugh? Okke Jaager, a Dutch pastor, wrote a booklet about "The Humor of the Bible." Can you suggest passages of the Bible which should be taken with a sense of humor?
10. Do you feel that the drama of life is a tragedy, or a comedy? If neither, how would you describe it? Is there more tragedy than comedy?

8   Games People Play

Eric Berne, in his book *Games People Play*, stresses that in every adult there remains some of the "spoiled child." Sometimes this is good, but often it is not because it shows the immature side of the adult. Too many adults act like children.

Many of the arguments in the home are on a childish level. A large number of people are emotionally unstable. They cope with the frustrations of life like a child. The fuse that controls temper is sometimes very short and temper tantrums are not uncommon. Some find that tears are an effective way of getting out of a tight spot.

A number of adults show their spoiled child traits by taking from others, but never giving. Overdependency is another indication of a childish relationship to others. Some husbands or wives have never let go of mother's apron strings.

But sometimes it may be good that there is something of the child left in all of us. Many people take themselves too seriously. There are times when we should take the carefree attitude of the child so that we can enjoy the little things of life more. It has often been said that a man is just an overgrown boy, but his toys are more expensive.

When we allow the child in us to take over we are going to have trouble. It is permissible for little boys to attack each other physically, but adult men get in trouble with the law when they do that.

Yet there are ways in which we must be like children. Our Lord told us that we should be like little children to enter the Kingdom. We are also told that we should grow in a spiritual way. This means that we must learn to control and conquer ourselves, our jealousies, our angers and hostilities, and our basic inner passions.

Some people betray their immaturity in the way they think about God. Many still seem to think of God as the man who sits on the throne and punishes people for all the wrongs they do. It is hard to learn to know Him as a Spirit, as a loving being and one who really cares.

You do not expect a teen-ager to have the kind of faith that should be found in a man of fifty. But it is tragic when a person of fifty has the kind of faith that you expect in an adolescent. An adult faith must match our years.

What the Bible Teaches

"To attain the measure of the stature of the fullness of Christ." Ephesians 4:11-14

Children play in the marketplace. Matthew 11:16-19

Exploring Our Feelings

1. We see a lot of immature people today. Why do people find it so difficult to grow up? Do you feel that our culture tends to make people more dependent and childish?
2. Tom Harris wrote a book entitled, *I'm OK, You're OK*. He tells us that there are four possibilities: "I'm not OK, but you're OK"; "I'm not OK, you're not OK"; "I'm OK but you're not OK"; "I'm OK, you're OK." Which of these presents the picture of a healthy adult? A healthy marriage? What is wrong with the other statements?
3. Jesus tells us that we should be like a little child to enter into the Kingdom. We are also told that we should not be childish. Is there some conflict here?
4. Eric Berne feels that many adults are playing games in the way they live with others, and especially in their marriages. He mentions the things people argue about, the way they solve their arguments, the jealousy that is present, the way they handle money and the way they face frustration. How do you react to this approach? How can we stop playing games and start living like adults?
5. What is wrong when the kind of faith you can expect from a teen-ager is seen in a person of fifty years of age? How should their faith be different?
6. What are the means given to us that help us to grow emotionally, in our relationships, and in our spiritual life? Do you observe any reason for a lack of outgrowing the child in us?
7. Do you feel that your church helps you to live a more mature kind of life, or does your church lead to greater feelings of dependency?
8. Is there such a thing as a healthy dependency on God?

9 What Is Love?

The word *love* is used a great deal in human speech. Many songs and poems are written about it, and yet it is hard to define the word. It means many things to many people. There is also a lot of confusion in the minds of people. When a wife is asked, "Do you love your husband?" she may answer, "I think so, but I'm not sure."

What some people call "love" may be a physical attraction or it may be a feeling of dependency or of mutual need. Such love usually does not last. This may be the reason why some seemingly "perfect marriages" break up.

Human love may be of two kinds. There is a love for its own pleasure, and there is a love for the sake of others. Self-seeking love lasts as long as the object of affection gives personal satisfaction and enjoyment. It is more interested in getting than in giving.

Unselfish love is hard to define. It requires the giving of ourselves to another, and this requires that we also feel that we have something that is worth giving to another. Paul sees love as having various qualities such as patience, kindness, generosity, humility, courtesy, unselfishness, sincerity, and honesty.

When children are brought up in a home where love is lacking they will fail to learn both to love and to be loved. Both of these are important, for they form one of the deepest needs of the human heart. Children who are strangers to love will find it very difficult to learn to love when they become older. This is one of the pathetic by-products of a broken home.

Love requires a sense of mutual trust. If we do not really trust others, if we feel that if we trust others we will get hurt, we miss the most important ingredient of a loving relationship.

The absence of love leads to a search for substitutes for love. A person who is sexually promiscuous, one who rebels against society, one who tries to gain attention by various forms of misbehavior, is looking for a counterfeit of love. Some people set their love on a dog or a cat.

The essence of the religious life is also the matter of loving and being loved. We feel the love of God for us, and we respond with love to Him. We love Him because He first loved us.

What the Bible Teaches

Paul's great hymn to love. I Corinthians 13
The love of God for us. I John 3

Exploring Our Feelings

1. If your daughter said that she is "madly in love" with a young man whom you feel would not make a good husband, how would you handle the situation?
2. A couple married for three years tell their pastor, "But we just don't love each other anymore." What is wrong?
3. A young wife was very dependent on her husband. She could not stand to have him go out for a hunting trip because she felt uncomfortable when he was unavailable. Is this an expression of love? How should her husband handle this?
4. After a couple was married for a few years, the husband began to drink very heavily and often abused his wife when he was drunk. Should she continue to love him under such circumstances?
5. How can parents show their love for their children without spoiling them? How would you handle your little boy if, after you spanked him, he said, "I hate you, because you don't love me anymore"?
6. In many churches there is an absence of real love among the members, or between the pastor and the church members. What can be done about this situation? How is it possible that there should be so much hatred between Christians?
7. Often, in the extended family such as mothers-in-law, brothers or sisters and their husbands, there is a great deal of lovelessness and competition. Is this a normal thing or is it possible for a whole family, including all the in-laws, to live in a loving relationship? How can this be developed?
8. How do we know that God loves us? Do we have to feel this? How can this be found?
9. Are we supposed to love all people? How is this possible?
10. Ministers are often accused of preaching too much about love. Do you feel that this is overdone? Why do people object to this?

10   The Way We Dress

When we first meet a person we usually make
a mental note of how the person is groomed and
dressed, for this gives an indication of the kind
of person we are dealing with. The way we dress
reveals a good deal about ourselves. Slovenliness
in dress and grooming indicates low self-esteem.

A person's pride is involved with the adornment of the body. There are some who tend to
"over-dress." This indicates that they do not
have much self-confidence for they want people
to notice their external appearance rather than
the inadequate person they feel they are.

Many people show that they do not like
themselves the way they are. They make exten-
sive use of wigs, hair coloring, and other forms
of physical makeup. Some want to hide their
real age. This is not wrong in itself but it does
reveal their inner feelings about themselves.

Since this is true, there must also be a Christian way to dress and to groom ourselves. It is
not required of us that we preserve the form of

dress of twenty-five years ago, but it does require that we dress in a tasteful way. We should not offend others but our appearance should reflect the Christian spirit.

Already in the days of Paul there was a tendency to lay too much stress on appearance and he warned that it is far more important to be concerned about the adornment of the inner person, "the hidden man of the heart."

Dress does not really make the man, or woman, but it does serve as an indicator of who and what we are. A number of schools have laid down regulations about the forms of dress that are permissible. Some churches require that a woman's head should be covered. In some churches a man would feel ill at ease if he did not wear a coat or jacket.

We are expected to conform to the standards set in certain communities and places. So it is not asking too much of a person to conform to certain patterns of good grooming as a Christian. A part of this grooming will include the grooming of his inner self, as he seeks to reflect the spirit of Christ which will give an unmistakable glow to his whole appearance and manner.

What the Bible Teaches

Inner adornment. I Peter 3:3-6
Adorned with good deeds. I Timothy 2:8-10

Exploring Our Feelings

1. Do you feel that it is true that a person reveals what

35

kind of person he is by the way he dresses and grooms himself?

2. How do you react to a person who dresses far younger than his age? What do you think of using hair coloring or wigs to hide the gray hairs?

3. Do you think we lay too much emphasis on personal appearance in our culture? Do you think that we do not stress enough the "inner man," or the adorning of our inner self? How would you maintain balance in these matters?

4. What is proper dress for a church service? Should women wear hats and men wear suit coats? Should the minister wear a robe?

5. Do you think a school has a right to set up a dress code banning short skirts or tight jeans? How would you feel about having all the children dress alike in some form of uniform?

6. Some people who live near one of our churches felt ill at ease there because they could not afford to have clothing equal to that worn by church members. Their children felt ill at ease in Sunday school because their shoes were not as good as those the other children wore. How do you feel about this?

7. If you saw a woman shopping in a discount store while wearing a fur piece, how would you react?

8. Should Christians follow the latest styles or should they tend to be a bit more conservative in dress?

9. Is there a Christian way of grooming and dressing?

10. What does it mean to "adorn the hidden man of the heart in the incorruptible apparel of a meek and quiet spirit"? (I Peter 3:4, ARV)

11 "Workaholics"

Some people are addicted to alcohol, others to drugs, and this is not socially acceptable. But many people are addicted to work and are praised by others, for this is well accepted in our culture. We all like to boast about the large amount of work we do, for this makes us feel good.

In school we all look for good grades and we measure our accomplishments by the number of "A's" we get. In business we boast of the amount of sales we make, or how much money we make. Some will boast that they need only five hours of sleep at night and label those who want eight hours as lazy and lacking in ambition.

But there are inherent dangers in the workaholic. Men are often too busy to spend time with their families. Some cut off all social contacts and they become "loners." Too much work also cuts out recreation and cultural enjoyments, and a person becomes rather dull and uninteresting.

The man or woman who gets lost in work is really insecure. He seeks approval not for who he is but for what he does. The insecurity becomes evident in the fact that these people boast about their accomplishments and feel that they must do a bit more than Dad or a favorite brother or sister did. That is a poor form of competitiveness.

The workaholic often reaches the breaking point in his health, either physically or emotionally. It is an unhealthy way to live. People often come into the hospital and say, "I have overworked myself." I do not believe that any person overworks. It is rather the fact of working under too much tension, or of having poor work habits.

When other people can make a living in forty hours per week, the workaholic is selling himself short because it takes him sixty to eighty hours per week. People who set material things as their primary goal are always in danger of becoming workaholics.

Life is like a wheel with four spokes: work, love, worship, and play. When one of the spokes is too long, the wheel will wobble through life. We must learn to keep life in balance.

Jesus tells us that a man's life does not consist in what he has, or in the amount of work he does, but in what he is. We need to develop habits of living that strengthen our character and give us opportunity to live a balanced life.

What the Bible Teaches

Description of a lazy man. Proverbs 6:6-11

Invitation to rest a while. Mark 6:30-32
Bodily exercise compared to godliness. I
Timothy 4:8

Exploring Our Feelings

1. Do you think that some people break down emotionally because of "overwork"?
2. Would you rather have a husband or a wife who is a bit on the lazy side, or would you rather live with a workaholic"?
3. Is it wrong for a person to work hard to get ahead in his position in the world? When does it become wrong?
4. We live in a very competitive world. Is this bad? What would be an unwholesome reaction to competition? We sometimes describe a person as being "competitive." Is that a good trait of character?
5. Evaluate this statement: Some men become workaholics so that they will have an excuse for being absent from their wives and children a great part of the time.
6. How about this one: Some people work extra long hours so that they do not have to get involved in social or church activities.
7. A father who had a regular job plus an extra job in the evening complained that his wife and children did not appreciate the fact that he was such a good provider for the family. What is wrong with this man? Or is there something wrong with his family?
8. In our world the measure of success is the income of a person. Some men are $10,000-a-year men, some are $25,000-a-year men. How do you like to be measured that way? What must be our standard of success?
9. Is there a Christian approach toward work? Is work only a secular activity?
10. What is the best way to deal with a person who is addicted to work?

12 The Lost Art of Conversation

God gave man the power of speech. This statement means more than the fact that God has given us the needed equipment to make words and sentences. To talk with people means to have a special relationship with them. We not only see and touch and feel others but we also communicate thoughts and concepts.

Today TV and the radio has largely taken the place of conversation. It is hard to find people with whom we can freely and confidentially converse, for many do not care to listen and others have very little to say.

When husbands and wives have little to say to each other, the relationship between the two breaks down. When parents cannot communicate with their children, or children with parents, the confidential relationship between the two is broken. People in the same family can become strangers to each other.

Dr. Louis Evans, in one of his books, writes about "table talk." He suggests that you can judge a family by the kind of conversation they have around the dinner table. It may be that they gossip, or perhaps they argue a good deal. Dinner time may be a time of fellowship and good conversation. It can, on the other hand, become a time of friction or fury.

If you are interested in people you will want to talk with them. It's good to learn to talk with strangers on a plane or bus, or in a casual setting. We should develop this art.

It takes time to regain the art of conversation. We should learn to direct the conversation into interesting channels. This requires that one also learns the art of listening.

Good conversationalists do not argue, they discuss. They are neither push-overs nor are they persons who know it all. They don't talk to people, or at people, but with people. They try to build up, rather than break down.

When you tell something about another person that is not favorable, ask first: Is it true? Then, is it kind? And also, is it necessary? This will eliminate gossip.

What the Bible Teaches

God is interested in our conversations. Malachi 3:16-18
Strong ideas about the use of words. James 3:6-12

Exploring Our Feelings

1. A husband and wife had difficulty communicating with each other. She would collect certain articles from magazines for her husband to read and then they would have something to talk about. What is your reaction to this arrangement?

2. How do you react to people who talk a great deal, who tend to monopolize the conversation? Why do you react in the way you do?

3. Today a good deal of emphasis is laid on "Conversational Evangelism," such as is used in coffee houses. Do you feel this is an effective way to reach others with the gospel? What would you talk about in such circumstances?

4. People today talk much more freely about sex than people in a previous generation. Is this a good thing?

5. Why do children find it difficult to talk with their parents about their problems? Do you think there is a communication gap in your home? How can you overcome it?

6. Many people find it easy to talk about the church, preachers, and teachers, especially to tell what is wrong with them. Why is it hard for many to talk about their own spiritual experiences?

7. Most of us talk more about things and persons than about feelings. Why? How can we learn to be more open with our feelings?

8. How do you react to a person who likes to argue? What is wrong with such people?

9. When does telling something about someone else become gossip? Is it wrong to gossip?

10. Do you think James is too harsh when he talks about the "sins of the tongue"?

13   The Misuse of Religion

There are a lot of people who misuse their religion and as a result their faith is not a vital factor in their life. Whenever one uses his Christianity for his own personal advantage it is an indication that all is not well with him.

Possibly the most common misuse of religion is among those who are hyper-religious. Such people inject a great deal of pious conversation into any subject under discussion. One hears much about "the way the Lord leads me." For example, "I feel that the Lord led me to come to see you." Some parents use the same approach with their children. They will pray with them when they have done something wrong instead of giving the offender a well-deserved spanking.

When the hyper-religious person is asked what he is doing about a particular problem or trying circumstance in his life, he will answer simply and pietistically, "I am praying about it." And that's that. All he does about his problem is pray. He expects God to do for him what he should be doing for himself. Religion, Bible reading, and prayer may never be a substitute for earnest soul-searching and hard work.

Some people use their faith as a cover-up for deeper inner feelings. When they become depressed that is an indication that their faith is low or that the devil is bothering them; at least that is the diagnosis they offer.

To use religion for our own personal gain does not show a high regard for the God whom we serve. God is not there just for our convenience, for our use; rather we are here to serve God and to love Him. The person who uses his religion to hide his real problems is not facing reality. That may even indicate laziness. Life's problems have to be solved where we meet them and God promises His blessing on our efforts.

A healthy religious life is expressed in a life of faith and trust. It will drive us to a life of devotion and loyalty to the Christ. We must seek for the ways in which faith leads to the health of both our souls and our emotions.

What the Bible Teaches

Faith without works is dead. James 2:17-26
A counterfeit Christian—a true Christian. I John 1:6-10

Exploring Our Feelings

1. Is it ever proper to say that a person is "hyper-religious"? Would it be better to say that such a

44

person is using his religious life in the wrong way? Can a person be too religious?

2. In a mental hospital one hears a lot of talk about religion. Is it true that some people become sick because of their emphasis on religion, or is this a symptom? Why do the thoughts of people turn to religion when there is illness?

3. Do you feel that praying with a child who has done something wrong is a good means of discipline?

4. "I believe in faith healing, but I do not believe in faith healers." How do you feel about that statement?

5. How do people cover up their angry feelings with religion?

6. Some people follow the teachings of the "new morality" on the basis of their religious beliefs. How do you react to this? (A couple who were having an extra-marital affair talked about the beautiful spiritual relationship between them.)

7. A person who is having a lot of problems, when asked what he is doing about it, says, "I have been doing a lot of praying about it." How do you react?

8. What is the difference between "using God" and "serving God"?

14   On Being Tactful

Tact is the skill of dealing with persons or difficult situations in a sensitive way, without giving offense. It is important for all who are interested in having good relationships with others to develop the use of tact. The approach we take to others can leave a pleasant impression or it can turn a friend into an enemy.

Paul made use of tact when he spoke to the people at Athens. He adapted his message to the people and their culture. It is well known that Christians can often be very tactless in the way they talk to others about the Christian faith. Some people have gained a bad impression of the church from the way people talk down to others.

There is need of a great deal of tact in family living. Husbands and wives often forget that even after years of marriage tact is needed to keep a marriage running smoothly. Parents often say some tactless things to their children.

One thing that requires a lot of tact is making

an apology, or offering a good excuse. When we deal with someone whom we have offended or someone who is angry we will have to choose our words carefully.

Being tactful does not mean that we have to sacrifice our convictions, or change our standards of living. It does mean that we are flexible enough to approach our fellowmen with courtesy and with concern. We may not run roughshod over the feelings of others.

It is possible to try to be so adaptable to others that we become spineless individuals, people who do not dare to express an opinion of their own. This is not being tactful, but merely fear that others will not accept us.

We may have to yield on some of the little things of life so that we do not irritate other people. It is more important to be concerned about the more important things in life, and this will require courage as well as tact. Paul says that he "became all things to all men," but goes on to say that it was his desire to "at least win some."

It is good to learn to be tactful, and then to practice it.

What the Bible Teaches

Tactful preaching at Athens. Acts 17:22-34
Dissatisfied people compared to children. Matthew 11:16-19
Great tact used at Jacob's well. John 4:9-26

Exploring Our Feelings

1. We are told to be honest. Is it possible to be completely honest and yet to be tactful?
2. Some Christians, including some ministers, will approach a person and say, "Brother, are you born again?" How do you react to this kind of question? Do you feel that this is a good way to witness?
3. A young lady met her friend and remarked that she did not feel that her friend's new hairstyle did much for her. Her friend was angry. If you were that young lady, how would you handle the situation?
4. A mother told her little boy, who was misbehaving, that he was very rude and that she did not like him that way. Is this using tact? How would you talk with him?
5. When you are late for an appointment, do you make an excuse? Do you give the right explanation? Or do you find some other tactful way out of the situation?
6. Do you like people who are always so polite that they never really express their feelings or ideas? Is there ever a time when we should be really blunt with others?
7. Is there really a tactful way to deal with very sensitive people? How do you approach them?
8. Do you think Jesus was tactful in His dealings with people? How about the way He talked to the Pharisees?
9. If a minister preaches a sermon that is very direct and to the point, some people take offense. If he preaches in a very tactful way, mentioning the sins of the people indirectly, he will be described as a weakling. How can a minister preach on some sensitive subject in such a way that he will not create enemies?

15   The Battle for Sunday

In our world today there are many people who do not observe the Lord's day. Many business places are open and do a thriving business. Sports events are scheduled for Sunday because the attendance is better on Sundays than during the other days of the week.

The battle for Sunday must be fought at various levels. The "blue laws" and Sunday closing laws are antiquated and hard to enforce. You can well expect this in an age when many do not make Sunday a day of worship.

A more basic battle for Sunday is in the church and the Christian community. The witness of Christians requires more than just attending worship services once or twice on Sunday. It is our duty to help those business concerns that close on Sunday.

Another battle for Sunday is in the home, and in our own lives. One man said, "I would rather lie in bed Sunday morning thinking about church than to be in church thinking about bed;

at least my thoughts are in the right place." Sunday is a nice day for the family to have recreation, to travel, and to just be together.

The result is that there is a changing attitude toward the Lord's day. It is important to take a positive approach, for this is what Jesus did. He did not lay down many rules, but He does want us to dedicate the day to the Lord of the Sabbath.

I would not like Sunday to be a day of many don'ts, for there is a danger that for children it becomes a day that they will dread, or even hate. There is room for enjoyment and pleasure. For the true observance of the Lord's day is more than spending time in church and Sunday school. It must be a day that is set aside for Him.

This will require a battle. If we are to keep this day "holy" as we have been commanded, we must seek for the things that bring spiritual advantages and enrichment. It must be a day of rest, but also a day of gladness. This may mean that we curb our own desires, and that we seek to promote things that will help our family.

The proper observance of Sunday will require a battle—but the result will be very much worthwhile.

What the Bible Teaches

The Sabbath was made for man. Mark 2:23-28
Remember the Sabbath day, to keep it holy. Exodus 20:8-11
The first day of the week. I Corinthians 16:1, 2

Exploring Our Feelings

1. Should we, as Christians, try to get laws passed by the city or state that regulate the kind of business that may be conducted on the Lord's day? If we do, are we fair to the Jews and the Seventh-day Adventists?

2. We feel that we may take a ride in our car on Sunday. Is it then wrong to take a boat ride on a lake, or ride on a snowmobile on Sunday? We may go for a walk, would it then be wrong to go for a swim? We have a large meal on Sunday noon. Would it then be wrong to have a picnic in the backyard?

3. Recently when I preached as a guest minister in one of our churches, the elders, in the meeting of the consistory before the evening service, excitedly discussed the football game they had watched on TV that afternoon. What should I have done about that?

4. Some people say that we have too many church activities on Sunday, so that it is no longer a family day. How do you feel about that?

5. Do you feel that Jesus was more lax in His teachings about Sunday observance than the Jewish leaders of His day? If the Sabbath is made for man, does this allow us to do what we feel is best for us?

6. Many churches today have only a morning worship service. Many people attend only the morning service even if an evening or afternoon worship service is scheduled. Why have two services? Why not just one? Why not three?

7. Next door to a man who usually mowed his lawn on Sunday lived a man who always went to church on Sunday. As the second man and his family left for church, they always exchanged friendly greetings, but he never said anything about the lawn-mowing bit. After a few weeks the first man said, "I know that you don't like it that I mow my lawn on Sunday, so I am not doing it anymore." Do you feel the Christian was an effective witness? Would it not have been better to have told his neighbor why it is wrong to mow lawn on Sunday?

16 Seeing Life Through Dark Glasses

There are people who are always looking at life from the dark side. Wherever they go they leave a little cloud of gloom. It seems that such people are most happy when they are sad or when they have something to complain about.

There are various things that depress them. The weather is a favorite subject because it is either too hot or too cold, too wet or too dry. The world situation also causes them to find reasons to worry for they are positive that things are getting worse as time moves on.

Another source of complaint is young people. The behavior of young people today causes them to feel alarmed. Just read all the terrible things young people are doing!

A favorite subject for gloom is the state of the church and religion. Preaching is not what it used to be and practices allowed in the church today are sure indications that conservatism is losing out.

The gloomy person can do a great deal of harm. Living with him can be very trying for the other members of the family. The person who sees life through dark glasses is not a pleasant person to live with.

All of life will be colored by the emotions that control us. The person who grieves for the loss of a loved one for a long period of time, the one who always has some pain that bothers, the one who sees only the shadows, these are the ones who allow life to be controlled by depressing emotions. They are basically unhappy people.

One who sees life in all this gloom is an angry person. If such a person would allow his real feelings to come to expression I am sure you would find a person who has never resolved his hatred . . . so he becomes lonely, and often feels sorry for himself.

In Genesis 42:35-38 we learn that Jacob was not very happy. However, notice that none of the things he really worried about were true to fact. Life is usually much brighter and much more pleasant than it appears to the person with dark glasses. Jesus encourages us to live hopefully, positively, and victoriously.

What the Bible Teaches

Jacob's worry expressed. Genesis 42:35-38
Jesus condemns excessive worry. Matthew 6:25-34

Exploring Our Feelings

1. Many people who have a gloomy outlook on life claim that they are being realistic, rather than pessimistic. What is the difference between the two? Is it wrong to be a pessimist?

2. If you happen to be a gloomy person is there anything you can do about it? What?

3. Do you think that it is good for the church to have among its members those who are critical and who point out the weaknesses and evils in the church? How can they help? How should they be dealt with when they harm the spirit in a church?

4. What effect will gloomy parents have on their children? Isn't it true that parents often tend to be too pessimistic while children and young people tend to be too optimistic?

5. We are encouraged to be honest about our feelings. Should we let our feelings determine our outlook on life? How is it possible for us to overcome the control that is exercised by our feelings?

6. What role does our anger play in determining our moods and our general outlook on life? Isn't it natural that we have angry feelings at times?

7. Do you feel that things are worse in the world today than they were ten or fifteen years ago? Why do you feel the way you do? Many people think that things are much worse. Do you agree?

8. It often seems that the news media report only the bad things—the wars and the violence—and entirely neglect the good and happy things. How do you react to this?

9. Jacob worried about several things that never happened. How often have you worried about something that never happened? Did it help much to worry about it? How do you cope with worry in your life? Be specific.

17 Dreaming Dreams

It has been said that "all the world loves a dreamer." This is not always the case for Joseph was not too popular in his family when he told them about his dreams. Still, it is good to have dreams. Some psychiatrists lay a good deal of stress on the dreams of their patients.

Children have a tendency to have daydreams especially in a classroom, or while doing their homework. A young lady may dream of marrying a tall, dark, and handsome man, but she may not attain her goal. We all need our dreams in life. Some of these dreams will become reality, some will not. The person who has no dreams will live a dull and aimless life. Dreams give goal and direction in life, they help us to live today, but to reach for higher goals for the future.

Dr. Martin Luther King spoke eloquently of his dream, but soon afterward he was struck down by a sniper's bullet. It is good for parents to have dreams for their children, since they want their children to reach higher goals than they themselves attained.

Too often our dreams are of a material nature. I know an older couple who dreamed of the days when the husband would retire. They planned to travel and enjoy life, but a year before his retirement he suffered a stroke. Now his wife pushes him around in a wheelchair. Even some of our most noble dreams are not fulfilled.

Some people have suffered many failures in life. They have seen many of their goals and ideals shattered. This can test one's courage, for one may feel that there is no use to keep trying. God has His way of testing us to bring out the inner strength of our characters.

I love the statement God makes about David when He told him that he would not be permitted to build the temple of God. "It was good that it was in thy heart." God noted with approval the noble desires, even though David was not allowed to reach the fulfillment of his dream.

It is good to have dreams for the future. Dreams can be exciting, but they can also be frustrating. But they make life worthwhile for they give a goal and a purpose for living.

What the Bible Teaches

The dreams of Joseph. Genesis 37:5
The promise at Pentecost. Acts 2:17
Daniel's dream. Daniel 7

David's desire to build a temple. II Chronicles
6:8, 9

Exploring Our Feelings

1. Do you feel that our dreams have the same meaning
as the dreams of the men of the Bible? Do they have
any value at all?
2. Children often daydream. How do you feel about
this? How do you feel about adults who still daydream?
3. Why do we need the kind of dreams Martin Luther
King talked about? What are some of the ideals and
goals we ought to have for our families?
4. Therapists will often ask patients about their goals
for the future, such as, "What do you really want
out of life?" What is so important about this?
5. The goals and ideals of many people are material-
istic—they would like to be rich, or have a lot of
things. Is there anything wrong with this kind of
dream?
6. Certain parents wanted their youngest son to be a
doctor. He wanted to be a mechanic. He failed in
one school, so they tried another one. How do you
react to such a situation? Are the parents mistaken,
or is the son just a rebel?
7. Some young men, and young women, have as a goal
to find an ideal wife, or husband. How do you react
to this?
8. When people feel defeated because of failures and
disillusionments, can you blame them for saying,
"What's the use, with my luck I'm bound to fail
again"? Are there some people who are failures in
life?
9. We need high spiritual ideals. What must be our
attitude when we do not reach the heights of spiritual confidence we would like to attain?
10. In the account of David's desire to build a temple,
God says "It was good that it was in thy heart."
Does this mean that it is better to have dreams that
fail than to have no dreams at all? Does God give us
credit for our intentions?

18   The Individual in the Great Society

In our computerized age we become numbers and statistics rather than individuals with names. Our social security number is used at the place of our employment and the same number is used to process our income tax returns. Our bank checks are posted according to number by large impersonal computers. If you are in the armed forces you are identified by a number. Even in a barber shop or bakery you become number twenty-four in line rather than a person with a name.

These conditions indicate that in the great society we lose a lot of our individuality as a person. Individual initiative and incentive are not rated highly. It is important that we fit into the smooth operation of the big machine. Many people are quite content with this arrangement for it rewards the average man. We know that there are good teachers and poor teachers but we do not reward those who seek to excel in their work. This is also true of ministers, bricklayers, and carpenters. We live by the law of averages, and pay scales are set accordingly.

Our schools are geared to meet the needs of the average student. As a consequence we do a poor job with both the exceptionally bright child and the dull child. Even within the church, especially the larger church, the individual is lost in the crowd.

It is little wonder that many begin to ask, "Who am I?" for when we become part of a larger routine we lose our sense of personal identity. We are placed in a group, and often into a certain category, and all people in the group are given a label. We are described as being liberal or conservative, leftists or rightists, black or white, and then people make a broad general statement which covers everyone in that category.

God created us to be individuals, created in His image, and assigned to a purposeful place in this life. God looks on us as individual persons, with personal responsibilities and qualities. God does not lose one person among the millions that live in the world. He knows each one by name. We must learn to see ourselves that way too.

Faith in God is a deeply personal matter; the expression of that faith in our Christian life is a personal matter. Our relation with others must be on a person-to-person level. Our thoughts, our feelings, our inmost desires are very important in this age, because they make us who we are.

What the Bible Teaches

Jesus seeks for the one sheep. Luke 15:3-7
"Thou art the man." II Samuel 12:1-15
"Neither bond nor free, neither male nor female." Galatians 3:28

Exploring Our Feelings

1. When a person says, "I am an individualist, I have learned to think for myself," how do you react to him? Is it really possible for a person to think for himself in our age?
2. In many of our more modern school systems they have an "ungraded class system" in which a child can move as fast or as slow as he wants to. Is this good? Or does a child do better if there is competition?
3. Why are there always people who do not like to conform to standards that have been set up by society? When a school sets up codes of conduct and dress there are always some who object. To what extent should we conform to the standards of the community?
4. In a world that is becoming more and more overpopulated there is not much emphasis on the individual person. Do you feel that Christianity gives a solution to this? How did Jesus consider the individual person?
5. What answer have you found to the question "Who am I?"
6. Why is it important today to stress the personal factor in our Christian faith and experience? How can we do this?
7. Some churches stress very strongly what the members may or may not do. Those churches set up standards as to what one should believe, how one should live, how to observe the Lord's day. How do you feel about this? Would you feel more comfortable in a church that stresses personal freedom?
8. What is wrong with being "just average"?

19   Followers and Leaders

Educators tell us that in every group or class there is a positive leader and a negative one. Both of them are eager to control the group. The negative leaders are interested in disrupting the group and starting trouble, while the positive leaders want to guide things in a constructive way. It is up to the teacher to learn to know who is trying to lead. This implies that there are always leaders and followers.

Marshal Montgomery, one of England's great generals, calls leadership "the capacity and the will to rally men and women to a common cause." This is true of the hostile leader of a street gang as well as of a leader in the church or nation. It has been said that leaders are born, not made. It is possible, though, to learn leadership when we are given the chance.

Today it seems that we do not have great and outstanding leaders in either the nation or in the church. It is true that many of the leaders of the past have been glamorized by the passing years.

It has been said that it takes a lot more to be a leader today since people are more highly educated and skilled.

We need leaders; we also need followers. There is, however, no place for blind followers, the kind of people who will follow a person whether he is wrong or right. Leaders are human, they can also be mistaken, they can be working for a cause which is destructive. We should not engage in hero worship.

We should be dedicated to a cause, rather than to a person. There are leaders among the Panthers or the Hell's Angels, but we would hardly accept all the things they stand for, or the methods they use to achieve their goals. We must use discretion if we are to follow a leader.

The other way in which we may escape the worship of a human leader is to accept Christ as the Leader and Commander of our lives. Then it is not a question of what some favorite minister or doctor says; rather, we seek to do the will of Christ.

What the Bible Teaches

Respect for national leaders. Romans 13:1-7
Be ye followers of them. Hebrews 6:12
Joshua the leader. Joshua 1:16-18

Exploring Our Feelings

1. Would you agree that today there are too many followers and not enough leaders? How does our generation contribute to this situation? Would it be good if we had more leaders?

2. Would you like to be a follower, or would you rather be a leader?

3. Parents are supposed to be leaders in the family. How can this best be accomplished? Should the husband always be the leader in the family?

4. What is the difference between being a leader and being a controlling person? What is wrong with trying to control your mate, or people around you?

5. How can a person develop healthy abilities in leadership? Some churches have leadership classes. Are they valuable?

6. When people love their pastor they are inclined to accept everything he says as being true and valid. Is this a healthy way to follow a leader? What are some of the dangers?

7. Today we tend to distrust people who are the leaders of our nation such as the president or members of Congress. Does this lead to a strong nation? Is it good that we criticize these men as much as we do?

8. We often speak about "our great presidents" such as Washington, Lincoln, Roosevelt, or Eisenhower. Were these men really so great? After all, they were only human. Should we honor them for what they have done? Do we also have a right to criticize them?

9. What does it mean to you that Christ is the Leader and Commander of your life? Does this mean that we are followers. Can we be leaders while we are followers?

10. The Bible tells us that we must honor those that have the rule over us. What does this mean to you?

20 The Measure of a Man

In this age when young people seem to be growing taller, the man who is small of stature is often lost in the crowd, and he becomes the butt of many jokes. He will most likely buy elevator shoes to make himself look taller. Smallness of stature is something over which we have no control.

But in the passing parade of life there is something that is far more disastrous than being a short person, or being petite. That is being a person who is small of character. Many great people have suffered much at the hands of petty souls. Joan of Arc was burned at the stake by people who could not see the greatness of her vision. Many people hated Christ because they were too narrow-minded to tolerate His teachings.

There are various ways in which we reveal our pettiness. The small-minded person is easily upset by criticism, the big person can accept it in good grace. People often get upset by little things because they are not big enough to see life in its broader aspects.

You can measure your size by the number of friends you have, or by the number of people you do not like. It is good to make a list of the people you like and those you do not like and see which list is the longer.

We can also measure ourselves by the way we can accept failures and disappointments. When the little person fails, he will blame somebody or something else. A big person admits his failures and then rises from his mistakes to greater heights.

The person who has lofty goals and ideals will reveal that he has a big view of life. He will also live constructively, and positively, rather than critically and negatively. The petty person is against many things, but he is not inclined to reach out and be *for* something.

Some small characters listed in the Bible are Jonah, the man who hid his talent, and the elder brother. The example of real greatness is Jesus. He had a big character, revealed in a big heart and a life that showed it. "For whosoever would be great among you, let him be your servant."

What the Bible Teaches

Becoming like a child. Matthew 18:1-4
Serving others is important. John 13:12-17

Exploring Our Feelings

1. It is often said that men who are small of stature will

65

Small person runs others down to build themselves up.

talk loudly and try to be extroverts. Do you find this to be true? How would you explain this behavior? Why do people discriminate by calling a short man "Shorty" but describing a girl as "petite"?

2. Some people are described as being "narrow-minded." What does this mean to you? How do people become this way?

3. What is wrong with a person who finds it hard to like people? What might cause a person to dislike more people than he likes? What qualities of character are needed to learn to like people?

4. We all have some immature qualities, although some people are more mature than others. Is anyone ever perfectly mature? Can we do anything to attain greater maturity?

5. The church, as well as society in general, has many critics today. Is this good or bad? How do you account for the fact that there are so many critics today?

6. Jesus is held up before us as an example of maturity. What are some of the qualities He showed that indicate this? What are the marks of His greatness?

7. If you had a child, especially a boy, who was very short in stature, how would you treat him?

8. How does one develop spiritual greatness? Can a person develop a mature faith as long as he remains emotionally immature?

21 How Often Must We Forgive?

To have a loving relationship with others requires that we must often forgive others. Peter asks, "How often?" for the Jewish law required a person to forgive seven times. Jesus tells us to forgive seventy times seven—for by that time you will have really learned the art of forgiving.

The unforgiving spirit implies that there is a resentment, a feeling of hatred or anger, and as a result we no longer really love the person who has hurt our feelings. The ability to be angry is deeply rooted in our lives. The ability to forgive is something we must learn.

In the church the unforgiving spirit is considered to be a sin, for it deprives a person of the joy of fellowship with another person. It is wrong for two persons who claim to be children of their Heavenly Father to live in hate or resentment. The goal of worship is reconciliation with both God and our fellowmen.

An unforgiving spirit is also a cause of poor mental health, for our angers and resentments often stand in the way of finding inner peace. It shows that a person is too insecure, too easily feels threatened. He has a "don't step on my toes" attitude toward life. He is overly sensitive to what others may do to him.

The suggestions of Jesus are that we take a free and open attitude toward the real or imagined hurts we have in life. We should be able to talk them out and in this way find as well as give forgiveness.

Some people have never learned to have a warm and vital relationship with others. They did not find this in their childhood, and they never learned it as they grew up. It is a mark of immaturity.

A good marriage requires grace as well as love. We must be able to forgive the failures of our mates. How often? Jesus says, "seventy times seven." By that time we will have truly learned to forgive.

What the Bible Teaches

How often must we forgive? Matthew 18:15-22
Loving God and loving our fellowmen. I John 4:19-21

Exploring Our Feelings

1. Two brothers who lived about a mile from each other had not talked to each other for four years

because they had a quarrel about a deal that involved fifty dollars. What is wrong with such people?

2. Should we always be ready to forgive others or are there times when this is asking too much of a person?

3. A married man had an affair with another woman. His wife took him back and said that she forgave him, but the relationship between the two was never the same. Did she really forgive? Suppose you were asked to give advice to this couple, what suggestions would you offer?

4. When husbands and wives have a disagreement should they give in to each other and just forgive, or should they try to work out their differences, even if it takes a few days?

5. If a child does something that is seriously wrong, should parents immediately tell him that he is forgiven, or should they let him sweat it out for awhile?

6. What causes some people to so easily take offence? Is this a spiritual problem or an emotional one?

7. When there is hatred and resentment between members in the church, should the pastor, or the consistory, get involved? If so, when?

8. What do you think of the practice in the church that requires people who are having trouble between each other to refrain from partaking of communion?

9. Why is it so hard for us to love some people?

22 The Gray Areas of Life

A pastor describes one of the members of his church as one "for whom there are only two sides to an issue: the wrong one, and the one to which he holds." I am sure we all know people for whom there are no gray areas in life, only black and white.

Such people are usually stubborn and rigid. They also tend to be insecure, for they are afraid to look at both sides of an argument. This might prove that they are wrong and they cannot bear to be wrong. They do not want to change, for change is always painful. And change we must because we are living in a time of change.

Husbands and wives may pull in opposite directions and scathingly accuse each other of being wrong. When you talk with them you realize that neither is completely right or wrong and the truth is somewhere in the middle between the two extremes.

Parents often look at things differently than their children do. Some parents feel that they are right, period. The younger generation is wrong, period. This brings about a good deal of the conflict between the generations.

The real problem is that many want to draw a neat line of separation between right and wrong, light and darkness. In life, this is not the case. There are gray areas where there can be differences of opinion, or where we have to learn to be flexible enough to accept the fact that the opinions of others are as valid as our own.

We should not be stubborn; nor should we be pushovers. We need to have opinions of our own but we must also respect the opinions of others. We may not condemn others just because their life style differs from ours in the thousands of minor details of everyday living.

Some truths stand firm because they are taught in the Bible. Some things are commanded, others are forbidden. Between these extremes is a large gray area where we have a right and a duty to choose. This requires that we be flexible and adaptable. It may mean at times we must say, "I was wrong." If our lives are controlled by the kind of love which is expressed in I Corinthians 13 not only will we be able to respect the ideas and views of others but we will also have the right to expect that others will accord us the same privilege.

What the Bible Teaches

Qualities inherent in love. I Corinthians 13:1-8 " . . . all things to all men." I Corinthians 9:19-23

71

Exploring Our Feelings

1. Why is it hard to like a person who is very rigid and stubborn in his outlook on life? Is this because we have some of these qualities ourselves?
2. Do you believe that the things we do in life are either right or wrong? Jesus said, "He that is not with me is against me."
3. Some people feel that it is wrong to smoke. How can we determine whether it is right or wrong, or a matter of personal choice?
4. There are many differences among people and churches as to what may be done on Sunday. Do you feel that it is better to be too strict rather than to be too lax about our Sabbath observance activities and attitudes?
5. How should we deal with people who are very rigid in their views of life? Should we argue with them or just accept them?
6. In conflicts between the older generation and the younger generation in the church, should the church cater to the younger element since they are the future of the church? Is it possible to avoid alienating either group and still maintain an effective witness?
7. Many of us have become used to living in a certain way because we have been brought up that way. Is it a good thing to follow what we have been taught, or should we learn to adjust to the changes that take place?
8. Paul tells us that love "suffers long and is kind, it is not easily provoked." Can we carry this too far?
9. Can people who see no gray areas in life be effective witnesses for the gospel?

23 The Church in the Suburbs

Much has been written about life in the suburbs, for a new culture has developed in those areas to which people have moved from the inner city. Today it is a status symbol of the successful young family to live in a ranch house in suburbia. Many new pressures have developed for those who live there.

This also presents a changing pattern for the church in the suburbs. The churches compete with each other to find the kind of architecture that will fit into the pattern of their community. Church life is geared to those who live there. The social and community aspects of the church are stressed.

There is a danger that the suburban church will develop the air of the country club rather than the house of God. It is the center of the community where breakfasts and dinners are served to reach the people. Spiritual life sometimes is rather superficial since, for many, it is the "in" thing to be a member of the church, or at least to send the children to the Sunday school there.

Since each suburb has its own zoning laws, it also has its own standards of living. In some areas you must build a home with a market value of at least $30,000; in others, worth at least $50,000. This can well bring snobbishness and exclusiveness to a community. When this status symbol carries over into the church, a most unhealthy situation exists.

The church in the suburbs may well be our largest frontier for evangelism. Due to the fact that there are people of varying religious backgrounds, and some with no religion at all, there is an opportunity to reach the "up and outs" rather than the "down and outs."

It seems that James would have made a good pastor for a church in the suburbs, although some of his blunt remarks might not be too popular in the average church today. We should heed his warnings; we should also accept his challenge—"Faith without works is dead."

What the Bible Teaches

A poorly dressed man comes to church. James 2:1-5
Bearing each other's burdens. Galatians 6:2-5

Exploring Our Feelings

1. Due to zoning restrictions only the people of a certain economic class can live in some suburbs. Do you feel that this also applies to the church in the

suburbs? Would it be more wholesome to have the rich and poor living together in one area? Why, or why not?

2. The flight to the suburbs is interpreted as a desire to escape the problems of the inner city. Would it not be better if Christian people would continue to live in the depressed areas of the city so that they can exert their influence there? Why, or why not?

3. Would the suburbs be a good place for a mission chapel? Why do many of our churches build their mission chapels at a considerable distance from the church? Is there room for neighborhood evangelism in the community of your church?

4. Would a poor person, not too well dressed, feel at home in your Sunday morning worship service? Would a child of such a home feel at ease in your Sunday school? Do you feel comfortable when someone like that attends?

5. Is life in the suburbs really better for the family, or do we use this as an excuse? There are also social problems in the suburbs. Why is this so?

6. Many writers state that there is a great deal of "status seeking" in the suburbs. Do you think this is true? How do you feel about it?

7. Do you think that the "morning coffee" often held in suburban communities is good? What might be some pitfalls of these gatherings?

24 Grasshoppers or Men

When the spies returned from investigating
Canaan they had a lot of good things to report.
It was a good and rich land, they even brought
some of the fruit as evidence. But they also saw
the Nephilim, the giants, and the spies felt like
grasshoppers in the sight of these sons of Anak.

These spies were correct when they said "we
seemed *in our own eyes* as grasshoppers in their
sight." Their personal viewpoint was wrong. The
problems of life look so big when we see ourselves in the light of our fears.

Too many people take the "grasshopper outlook" in life; they feel so insignificant and are
sure they will fail. This feeling displays not only
a lack of faith, it also shows a poor mental
attitude. Such people are defeatists for they
feast on failure rather than build on their successes.

This is an unrealistic view, for no one suc-
ceeds 100 percent of the time and no one fails
100 percent of the time. Failures help to keep us

humble, whereas success encourages us to move ahead confidently. We all have failures—it's our attitude toward them that counts.

Thomas Edison made four hundred models of his incandescent bulb before he found one that would work. All scientific discoveries have come by trial and error; there were failures before there was success. Failures should be viewed as challenges rather than as reasons to quit trying.

We often say, "I can't" when it would be more correct to say, "I'm scared." The matter of facing problems in society, in the home, in our work, or in our own lives requires a sense of confidence in ourselves. Like the spies, we tend to compare our own size with that of the giants. Instead, we should make use of the inner strength that comes when we measure our frustrations alongside the inexhaustible resources of God.

Psalm 37 presents four ways of conquering our fears:

Verse 2 "Trust in the Lord."

Verse 3 "Delight thyself in the Lord."

Verse 4 "Commit thy way to the Lord."

Verse 5 "Rest in the Lord."

What the Bible Teaches

The spies' report. Numbers 13:27-33
God's prescription for anxiety. Psalm 37:3-7

Exploring Our Feelings

1. We all have fears. Is this wrong? When are fears healthy? When are they sick?

2. Do you feel that the "grasshopper attitude" toward life shows a lack of faith, or is this a part of our personality? How can we combat this attitude?

3. How do you measure success in your life? What do you mean when you say that one is a successful person? What do you mean when you say that one is a failure?

4. Some people brag a good deal about their successes in life. How do you feel when you are in the presence of such people?

5. When you are asked to do something and you say, "I can't do it," what are you really saying about yourself?

6. Many people are excessively dependent on the approval and recognition of others. What is wrong with such people? What can we do to overcome this in our own lives?

7. Do you think that "The power of positive thinking" is a good answer to the feeling of failure we often have? Do you think that it works?

8. The ten spies were rebuked for their lack of faith. Does faith in God really help us to conquer our fears? Will a sincere Christian live with a fear of failure?

9. Have you found a good way to handle your fears and frustrations in the face of failure? Share your way of conquering them with the rest of the group.

25   Are We Listening?

God gave men two ears and one mouth. If we follow this proportion we should be doing a lot more listening than talking. I fear that this is not the case, for many have never learned to listen. I often get the impression that when I am talking with a person he is thinking about what he is going to say next. I find this quite annoying.

The absence of the art of listening is a serious threat to the relationship between people, especially in the home. A little boy comes home from school and says, "I hate my teacher." The mother tells him that he may not say that. A daughter comes home late from a date and her father does not listen to her excuse but says, "There are no excuses." Then he proceeds to lecture her. He has not listened to her, so she most likely does not hear what he says.

One of the big problems in marriage is that couples do not hear what the other is really saying. Many people who need to talk out their feelings find it difficult to find someone who is willing to listen. Most helping agencies have a long list of people waiting to get a chance to talk out their problems.

It is important to hear more than the words people are saying. We must listen to what they are really trying to convey. We should try to find out their feelings and inner thoughts. Parents often have not really listened to their youngsters. The whites have not really listened to the blacks. Ministers often do not really listen to their church members. So we are all answering a lot of questions that people are not asking. And the real questions go unanswered.

This "tuning out" often leads to the communication gap between people and between generations. If we cannot hear each other when we are talking about the everyday relationships of life, how can we expect people to hear us when we talk about the spiritual and emotional aspects of living?

Many arguments grow out of the fact that we have not really been listening to each other. It is told of Abraham Lincoln that he said about one of his presidential aides, "I must get to know that fellow better because I am beginning to hate him."

When we learn to listen to others, others may be willing to listen to us.

What the Bible Teaches

"Hear me patiently." Acts 26:3

"How shall they hear without a preacher?"
Romans 10:14
"He that hath ears to hear, let him hear."
Matthew 11:15

Exploring Our Feelings

1. In some families the children seem to dominate the conversation at the dinner table. How would you react to this? Do you agree with the maxim, "Children should be seen and not heard"?

2. Why are there so many people today who need someone to whom they can unburden their feelings? Why can you talk more freely with one person than with another?

3. Why does a Christian need someone human with whom he can talk out his problems? Isn't it enough to just tell God about it in our prayers? Does it help to tell God?

4. They talk about the "art of listening" as one of the qualities of a counselor. What is this art of listening? What characteristics does it require? What does it mean to "listen with a third ear"?

5. We all go through a period as we grow up when we cannot talk to our parents about our problems. What causes this? Would it be healthy if a daughter of eighteen would confide all her thoughts to her mother?

6. Do you think that people really hear everything a minister says in his sermons? What parts of a sermon do you really hear?

7. Why is it harder to talk about spiritual things with our children or our mates than it is to talk about these things with other people?

8. What is the value of group therapy? Do you think that everyone could benefit from group therapy? Do you feel that sensitivity groups have value? Why do some people object to them?

9. Paul tells us to "rejoice with them that rejoice and to weep with them that weep." How does this help a person?

10. What does Jesus mean when He says, "He that hath ears to hear, let him hear"?

26 Hindsight or Insight

We have all said at one time or another, "Hindsight is better than foresight." This no one can contradict. "If we had only known!" is a complaint as empty as it is fruitless. Yet one may learn from past experiences.

Often psychiatrists and therapists lead a patient back to his childhood so that he recalls the experiences that contributed to his illness or maladjustment. It helps us to know how we got where we now are. So the real value of hindsight is that it may lead to better insight into ourselves.

"Know thyself" is the wise counsel of philosophers. Because of the complexity of man, no one really understands himself fully. David asked God to "Search me, and . . . know my heart." His goal was to know himself better.

The lack of progress in developing good behavior and rooting out bad behavior is caused by our tendency to so easily excuse ourselves by saying that our failings are just a part of being human—or an inherited trait. Then, even though we look back into our lives and see our failings, we do very little about them.

It's good to think about ourselves as we are, not just as we ought to be. This helps us to gain insight. Looking into the past can help us grow and develop some of the qualities we would like to have. We need this to become the kind of persons we would like to be. But gaining insight requires honesty and a lot of hard work.

And it's hard to be honest with ourselves—to really admit that we have traits of character that we should eradicate. It's easy enough to say, "I know I have many faults and sins," but sometimes it is difficult to name even ten of them!

It's good to look back, not to blame or condemn ourselves or our environment, but with the intention of gaining greater insight into both our strengths and weaknesses. Acknowledging these is the first step in developing our characters and personalities.

Spiritually, also, it is good to look back, not to punish ourselves for our past acts, but to live more victoriously in the present.

What the Bible Teaches

"Search me, O God, and know my heart . . . . "
Psalm 139:23, 24
"Forgetting the things that are behind, I press on." Philippians 3:12-16

Exploring Our Feelings

1. "If I had only known the situation in my husband's

family, I never would have married him." What is the feeling you get from this remark? What value does it have?

2. How can we get to know ourselves as we really are? Do you think a person ever reaches this ideal?

3. There are people who have done some pretty bad things in their lives, and they continually bring up this fact. Is this good for a person? What does this show about an individual?

4. Some people feel that God forgives them, but they find it hard to really forgive themselves. How can a person get over that feeling? How can we help such people?

5. Most people that are grieving because of the loss of someone close to them will live with regrets. "If I had known that he was going to die, I would have treated him better." "If I had known that my daughter was going to be killed in an accident, I would not have allowed her to go out." How do we handle this feeling of regret in grief?

6. Paul tells us to "forget the things that are behind." What are some of the things we ought to forget? Is it really possible to forget things that have happened to us in the past?

7. Psychologists tell us that some people seem to enjoy punishing themselves. Why would a person want to do this? What can you do to help him?

8. What does it mean to you when you pray this prayer of David, "Search me, O God, and know my heart"? Have you ever felt that you did not really dare to pray that prayer? How does God answer this prayer?

27 On Easy Street

After Solomon died, his son Rehoboam was unable to unite the nation. Jeroboam successfully led a revolt against Rehoboam. Although the nation was divided politically, it was still united religiously and Jeroboam realized that his authority might be endangered if the people of his kingdom continued to go to Jerusalem to worship in the temple. Accordingly, he built two golden calves and said, "It is too much for you to go to Jerusalem." He offered an easier religion.

There are many people on easy religion street. They like a religion that does not cost much in effort or money. A religion that does not cause much trouble or sacrifice appeals to the hearts of people.

But nothing worthwhile is ever gained on the easy road. To gain an education, to develop a talent, to learn a skill, or to build a constructive life always costs a great deal of effort. An athlete will not keep in shape unless he works at it constantly.

There is a danger in raising a whole generation that is looking for the easy way out. Many parents unconsciously encourage this by sparing their children the hardships they themselves endured. People naturally want to live as comfortably as possible.

Many men have tried the easy road. Raphael the painter and Edgar Allen Poe the author are only two examples. The Bible tells of others: the rich young ruler, the early life of John Mark.

I find it hard to believe that God would send His Son to the cross to atone for our sins, and then would lead the sinner to glory on flowery beds of ease. He still requires the broken spirit and the contrite heart. He still demands a surrender of the self and wholehearted devotion to His service.

Living on easy street doesn't contribute to strength of character. Jeroboam, for instance, is known as the man "who made Israel to sin." Today easy religion leads to easy morals, to a weakened structure in the church.

Possibly this is the reason God sends difficulties, wars, sickness of the body or mind, spiritual struggles. These are the things that strengthen our characters and build up our faith in a loving God.

What the Bible Teaches

Jeroboam's easy religion. I Kings 12:25-33
"Whom the Lord loves, he chastens." Hebrews 12:4-11

Exploring Our Feelings

1. How would you like to be a member of a church that tells you that it's easy to be a Christian? Do you find it easy?
2. Some churches have special golfer's worship services, so that those who want to play golf on Sunday need not miss church. What is your feeling about this?
3. Many people today do not like to hear doctrinal sermons. Is this because such a sermon requires more effort on the part of the audience? Would it be better to make every sermon practical?
4. Pierre Burton writes about the "comfortable pew." Do you find that it is comfortable to attend worship services? Should you be uncomfortable in church?
5. How do you feel about parents who do not want their children to suffer the same things they did when they were youngsters? One father said, "I used to walk to school even in the coldest weather. I am not going to let my children go through such an ordeal."
6. Some people say that it is much more enjoyable to them to listen to a service by way of the radio. How do you react to this? Why do so many churches broadcast their services?
7. Why do so few of our people really put forth the effort to learn to play an instrument such as the organ or the violin, while many learn to play the guitar?
8. Education at school is made much more pleasant and interesting for youngsters today, since newer methods are used. Is it good to make it easier for children to learn, or would it be better to require more effort?
9. What is the greatest test for a person, prosperity or adversity? What are some of the temptations of each of these?
10. Do we have idolatry today? Mention some of the idols that are common to us.

28   Job's Counselors

Dr. Wm. E. Hulme in his book *Dialogue in Despair* calls attention to the three friends of Job who come to comfort him as he sits on the ash-heap of despair. Job faced a real problem, but he was also a man with a strong sense of his own inner righteousness. It was not easy to shake him.

Two of his friends tell him that there must be something wrong in his life, he must have committed a terrible sin, for God would not send this suffering if he were a righteous man. They are a bit heartless, but they are concerned for Job. In their attack they pour vinegar into Job's wounds.

Elihu is a wiser counselor. He shows more love and understanding. He tries to lead Job into a deeper and better understanding of himself. Elihu does this by a spirit of acceptance. He does not ridicule Job. He tries to meet Job where he is.

Then Elihu tries to lead Job to a personal

confrontation with God. He wants Job to have a wider view of God and to see that God is sending these trials with a redemptive purpose. He leads Job to the place where he can say "when He has tried me I shall come forth as gold."

It is this kind of confrontation that all people need. There must be the place where a man really meets himself, and learns to know himself. Then also there must be a place where a man meets God, and feels the marvels of His love.

Many people struggle with the mystery of suffering. Many answers are given. People will often say, "If you only had more faith." But this does not help greatly to solve the riddles of life. It often muddies the waters and makes it harder to find our way out.

When we are confronted by a personal God, we may not be able to find answers to our "whys" and "wherefores." But it will help us to see Who guides our lives, and to know that His love and grace will never fail us.

It is important to see life as being purposeful. God does not work in a haphazard way; He always has a plan and a goal. It is not until we fall in line with God's purposes, God's will, that the load is lifted and the light shines through.

What the Bible Teaches

The climax of Job's journey into faith. Job 23:3-10

Exploring Our Feelings

1. The three friends of Job sat with him for seven days without saying a word. How would you feel if you were Job? What value or comfort is there in such a silence?

2. The charge of the counselors of Job was that he must have committed some sin, and for this reason he suffered. There is a relationship between sin and suffering. What is it?

3. If people had a stronger faith in God would there be less suffering and fewer patients in mental hospitals?

4. Why is it important that a person learn to know himself? How can sufferings and testings in life help us to a better self-understanding and awareness?

5. Suffering can be a punishment, a chastisement or a testing. Which of these three do you feel describes the sufferings of our generation?

6. Do you feel that God ever punishes sinners today?

7. A man who was rather profane and never attended church was told by a pastor that the Lord would punish him for the kind of life he lived. A year later a little child in that family was killed in an accident. The pastor told him that this was a punishment for his sin. How do you feel about this?

8. When God tests us, is the object for us to show God how much we love Him, or to show ourselves the strength of our love for God?

9. When a person grieves deeply, possibly more deeply than is normal, does this show a lack of faith? Or is this an indication of emotional disturbance?

10. What kind of counselor do you like best, one who is somewhat soothing and comforting, or one who is confronting and direct? What does this show about your attitude toward yourself?

29 Writing Our Own Commandments

As part of the worship of freedom, a number of people have written their own ten commandments. Such action rebels against the thesis that there is an objective standard by which all men should live. When man invents his own morality we get moral freedom and usually moral chaos.

Here are a few of man's commandments: "Thou shalt know no fear, for fear destroys life and cripples the soul." "Thou shalt have no unwanted children, for every child has a right to be wanted by healthy parents." "Thou shalt be strong and thy wrath shall be as the hurricanes upon the destroyers of life."

All of these commands concern human relationships. They have lost the vertical aspects of living. They do not take God into account. The healthy person does not need to write his own laws, he doesn't have to set his own standards of living. Society could not long exist if we laid aside the ten commandments of Sinai.

Many people, even though they do not write out their commandments, live as those who do. They will be honest as long as honesty pays. They live entirely by the pleasure-pain principle. Whatever gives enjoyment is good, whatever causes pain must be avoided.

Churches also have a tendency to set up their own rules and their own standards of what is right and wrong. Little room is left for freedom of choice. The Pharisees did that, too.

But it is well to note that freedom also demands responsible behavior. We are not free to do as we please. Having a friend will rob us of some of our freedom. Marriage brings responsibilities as well as benefits and pleasures. The worship of freedom leads to selfish and self-centered living.

We are all responsible for our actions. Even our immaturity is a sin, for we are not doing what we should be doing.

True freedom is found only in Christ. As new creatures in Christ we are no longer under the law but under grace. We are then free to live as responsible human beings, dedicated to the ideals and goals God sets for us.

What the Bible Teaches

Freedom in Christ. John 8:31-36
Freedom but not license. I Peter 2:16
Christ set us free. Galatians 5:1
Freedom and concern for others. I Corinthians 8:9-13

Exploring Our Feelings

1. For what reason would a person want to write his own set of ten commandments?
2. All of us, in a measure, set our own standards for our behavior. Is this wrong? Some people feel more free than others to do certain things on the Lord's day. Can we be too strict about Sunday observance?
3. Some schools have set up codes of dress and behavior. Does this infringe on the freedom of the students? Is this a good thing to do?
4. Today people take a far more permissive attitude toward behavior between the sexes. Do you approve of this?
5. How do you feel about the commandment quoted above, "Thou shalt have no unwanted children?"
6. It is often emphasized that it is better to take a positive approach than a negative one. The Ten Commandments are negative. Would it be better to take the more positive statements from the New Testament than to read the Old Testament commandments in our services?
7. Don't you think that Paul carries this idea of personal obligation rather far when he says that he would not eat meat if it caused his brother to stumble?
8. Is anyone free to do as he pleases?
9. Do you think that greater freedom for our children in the family helps to produce youngsters who are more secure, or less secure? Do you like permissiveness in the home?
10. What does it really mean to be "free in Christ"?

30 Happiness Is . . .

When we see the word *happiness* it brings to mind a variety of mental images. They come up from the memories of past moments of happiness and joy. It is good to find out what things give us a sense of pleasure, for this knowledge will help us to live with more joy in our lives.

There are many people who find happiness only when they are comfortable, when things go their own way. Such people are like children. They are immature, for their attitude reveals they are ruled by external circumstances. When things are pleasant and peaceful one is happy. When circumstances are unpleasant one is sad.

Something in the human spirit makes a person happy. Happiness must come from within. There are people who have many problems and yet they have a sense of inner joy. This possibly accounts for much happiness for although pleasure is found in things and events, joy is not.

Pleasure thrives on change. It may be very pleasant to make a trip of a hundred miles but it becomes a burden to travel a thousand miles. You laugh when you hear a joke for the first time but the second or third time it bores you. Grandparents are happy to see the grandchildren come but after a few hours it is good to see them go. Pleasure is fleeting; real joy is lasting.

Some people are naturally more happy than others. Some people always seem to be sad. Our early experiences and our training in our youth have a lot to do with our attitudes. But happiness is also something that can be developed. Happiness depends on our attitudes toward life's experiences.

Much depends on what we understand by *happiness*. For some people this may mean a loud and exciting party; for others it can mean a quiet evening reading a book. For some it is the excitement of the city, for others happiness is found in the quiet of camping at a lake or in the mountains. We express our personality by the things that make us happy.

Today many people seem to be unhappy. Many people take a grim outlook on life. Not a few of the modern songs and poems are sad. Often we hear, "What is there to be happy about in a time like this?"

Paul tells us to rejoice in the Lord always. This call to rejoice speaks of a true sense of happiness, for it comes from within and grows out of a relationship with God.

What the Bible Teaches

Rejoice in the Lord. Philippians 4:4-9

Rejecting the pleasures of Egypt. Hebrews 11:25
Shouting for joy. Psalm 5:11
"The fruit of the Spirit is . . . joy." Galatians 5:22

Exploring Our Feelings

1. How would you answer the person who says that there is nothing to be happy about today? Or do you agree with him?
2. What are the things that give you happiness?
3. Should a person always be happy, or are there also times when happiness is out of place?
4. Mention some of the things that rob us of our happiness. Are these real, or are they just an excuse?
5. How can we help our children to develop a joyful way of living?
6. Do you think that attendance at church tends to make people rejoice, or does it make people sad? Why are there so many, "long faces" among Christians?
7. Why do many older people lose their sense of humor?
8. Many people take themselves too seriously. What is wrong with this and how can you overcome it?
9. Some people seem a bit silly because they are always laughing or smiling. How do you react to such people?
10. Paul was in prison when he wrote to the church, "Rejoice in the Lord, again I say rejoice." How could a man really rejoice under those circumstances?

31 The Process of Growth

The process of growth is a remarkable thing. You can hold in your hand a tiny seed that is capable of becoming a tall plant with beautiful flowers. You hold a baby in your arms and you think of the potentials of that life as it grows and develops. There are various directions in which a person's character and personality must grow.

Like plants and trees we must grow in depth. We must become more deeply rooted. This requires that we learn to know ourselves better, gain insight into our strengths and weaknesses, and seek to find out what must be our place in this world.

We must also grow in an upward direction. We must always be seeking new heights for accomplishment, new goals for living, and new ideals for advancement. The Bible tells us that we must become more like the image of God as seen in Christ.

We also need to grow in breadth, reaching out

in an ever widening circle to others. Some people live very small lives because they find it hard to make new friends, or to live with people of a different race, national background, or religion. They have a stunted social growth.

In the process of growth we also have to outgrow some of the things that restrict us. Children outgrow their shoes or clothes. We must outgrow our childish behavior, immature reactions to life, our temper tantrums and hostilities and our fears and anxieties. All of life must be brought under the control of the higher powers of the soul.

Various agencies help us to grow—the home, the school and the church. Often these agencies are not as effective as they should be. The basic responsibility for growth, however, lies within ourselves.

I get the feeling that for some people it is very painful to grow up, for this means accepting the responsibility of facing life as adults, and it is easier to continue to be like children. Growth in one area of life—the spiritual—can be a great help in all other areas. To grow in the "grace and knowledge of our Lord Jesus Christ" gives us a sense of direction, but it is also a motivating force that will enable us to reach constantly to newer and more satisfying ways of living.

What the Bible Teaches

The growth of Jesus. Luke 2:52
Grow unto salvation. I Peter 2:1-3
Grow in grace and knowledge. II Peter 3:18

Exploring Our Feelings

1. Many people do not grow very much. How would you explain this—is it laziness? fear of responsibility involved with growth? lack of motivation?
2. Which of the three agencies, the home, the school or the church, is the most important for growth in our lives? If we have not experienced much progress can we blame these agencies? Why, or why not?
3. How do you feel about the statement that a lot of the problems of relationships with others is due to a "stunted social growth"?
4. What have you found to be the most helpful way to grow spiritually?
5. How can illness or some other trouble in life become a means for growth in our Christian character? Does illness always have this result?
6. I sense that there are many people in the church who have a feeling that they have "arrived." They do not feel that they need a great deal of growth anymore. How would you help such a person?
7. Parents often say to their children that they are wiser than the younger generation, while children often feel that they know as much as their parents because they have a better education. How would you answer a teen-ager who tells you this? How would you answer the parents?
8. Should anyone ever be fully satisfied with the position he has achieved? Should we feel satisfied with our spiritual progress? Should we be satisfied with the amount of knowledge we have?
9. What does it mean to you that we must "grow into the fullness of the stature of Christ?"
10. Jesus grew in "wisdom and stature and in favor with God and man." How was this possible for Jesus, the Son of God?

32   What Is Your Goal?

Much of the restlessness and tension in our age is born out of a lack of worthwhile purposes in life. Many people do not know just what they would like to get out of living. Many college students have not yet decided on a career, and some who have graduated have very ill-defined goals.

One of the big words in today's vocabulary is *success*. Each person wants to be successful in the work he is doing. In business this is often measured in terms of dollars and cents. A teacher or minister usually measures his success by popularity. It is more difficult to measure success as a parent or in being a friend.

There are some who have unrealistic goals. High school seniors often ask, "How long must I go to school to become a psychiatrist?" Such a goal is unrealistic for someone who is already tired of going to school before he reaches college. In choosing a career one must consider his natural aptitudes. Not everyone is cut out to be an artist or a public speaker or a professional athlete.

We must help our children set reachable goals, otherwise we will doom them to tension and frustration. Most of us need immediate goals as well as more distant ones. We have to think of the next step we are to take as well as the "distant scene." We have to face life in sections we can handle.

We are often told that we must "think big" if we want to accomplish great things. But a person who has suffered a few failures finds it hard to reach very high for fear he will fail again. Some people find failure very incapacitating.

Tension builds up in people who do not have adequate goals. With no real direction in life they flounder about, never feeling quite satisfied with themselves. This is often the result of lack of encouragement from parents or teachers in their formative years.

Jesus sets before us one of the loftiest goals of all when He says, "Seek ye first the kingdom of God." This must always be the great goal; the lesser goals will then fall into their proper places. This great goal will not be a substitute for other worthwhile goals; rather, it will help us make our choices in the proper setting.

What the Bible Teaches

Daniel purposed in his heart. Daniel 1:8
"Seek ye first the kingdom of God." Matthew 6:33

The love of Christ constrains me. II Corinthians 5:14

"I have fought the good fight." II Timothy 4:7, 8

Exploring Our Feelings

1. How would you finish this statement: "A successful parent is one who . . . . " How do you measure the success of a minister? of a teacher?
2. Do you feel that parents should encourage their child to become a doctor, or a professor, or a minister? Is it wise for parents to just let the child choose his own level in life?
3. In business a man is judged pretty well on the basis of the profits he makes. Are there other standards of success that should be used?
4. Why is it important for a person's mental health that he has some goal and purpose in living? What can you do about it if you do not have a definite goal?
5. One of the marks of immaturity that is often mentioned is that a person is not able to persist in reaching some goal in life. Such persons do not have the ability to persevere. Why are some people that way? How can we help them?
6. A man has as his goal to become a millionaire before he is fifty years old. What do you think of him? Would you like to be his wife? his child? his secretary? Why, or why not?
7. Our society is a very competitive one. Often success for one person means failure for another. How do you react to competition? Does it frighten you or does it bring out your fighting instinct?
8. What does the statement of Jesus, "Seek ye first the kingdom" mean for your life? Is that possible in today's world?
9. A man seemed to be very successful in his business, everything he touched seemed to turn to gold. He was in some ways a genius. Yet he was a very unhappy person. Why should he be so depressed? Do you feel that you would be depressed under such circumstances?

33 Living Victoriously

We may describe a person as one who is making a poor adjustment to life, or a marginal adjustment; or we may say that he is well adjusted. This emphasizes the fact that people make adjustments. The Bible speaks of living victoriously, even of being "more than conquerors."

The victorious life requires first of all that we learn to conquer ourselves. We must get ourselves under control. This means that we learn to face life with its temptations and frustrations, and come out victors rather than victims. It requires a lot of grit to overcome our hostilities and anxieties. This means that we must overcome the spoiled child in us and learn to live as adult Christians.

The victorious life also means that we live positively. There are too many who face life negatively; they stress the "don'ts" rather than the things they should do. The victors have ideals and goals, and they reach for them with all their powers.

The victorious life also requires us to live constructively. There are tremendous opportunities for all of us today if we will only roll up our sleeves and get to work fulfilling our roles adequately. Today there are too many negative critics, people who see much that is wrong. A building, or a home, or a church which has taken many years to build can be broken down in a very short time.

To live victoriously we must live enthusiastically. Aimless living leads to boredom. Faith in God and love for Christ drives one to work for His cause. The twelve apostles were sparked with an enthusiasm that drove them to preach Christ to their generation regardless of what it cost them personally.

Many people today, infected with defeatism, question the worthwhileness of the struggle. Faith in a victorious Christ, however, assures us that even though we may lose a battle now and then, ultimate victory lies ahead.

Victorious living gives a sense of personal satisfaction and joy, something we all need. Too many people find the religious life a somber thing that lacks the real joy they should find there. Such people have lost sight of the fact that already in this life they can find a sense of victory as they look forward to the eternal victory they shall experience.

What the Bible Teaches

Being "more than conquerors." Romans 8:37-39

"Faith is the victory." I John 5:4
"I have overcome the world." John 16:33

Exploring Our Feelings

1. How do you feel when people say that they have made a poor adjustment to life, or a marginal adjustment? What does this mean to you?
2. We must learn to conquer ourselves. What does this mean to you? Does this also mean that we must conquer our anxieties?
3. We are often tempted to sin. What can we do about it? God promises that we will not be tempted beyond that which we can bear; if this is true, how do we fall into sin? Does this mean that we are not strong enough?
4. How do you like negative people? Why do we develop that spirit?
5. There are many protest groups today. Would you join in with protest marchers? Under what circumstances should we protest? How about protesting against things that you think are wrong with the church?
6. A child is born with enthusiasm. If he loses it this is because something has dampened it. Does this account for a lack of enthusiasm in many people today?
7. Why do older people have a tendency to have less drive and enthusiasm than younger people?
8. Each person has something different that calls forth his enthusiasm, for example, some people are enthusiastic about their work, others about sports, some about getting ahead. What does the object of our enthusiasm tell us about ourselves?
9. How does our faith help us to be victorious? Does our faith always do that for us?
10. Jesus says, "I have overcome the world." According to human standards He was a failure, not a success. To what kind of victory do these words of Jesus refer?

105